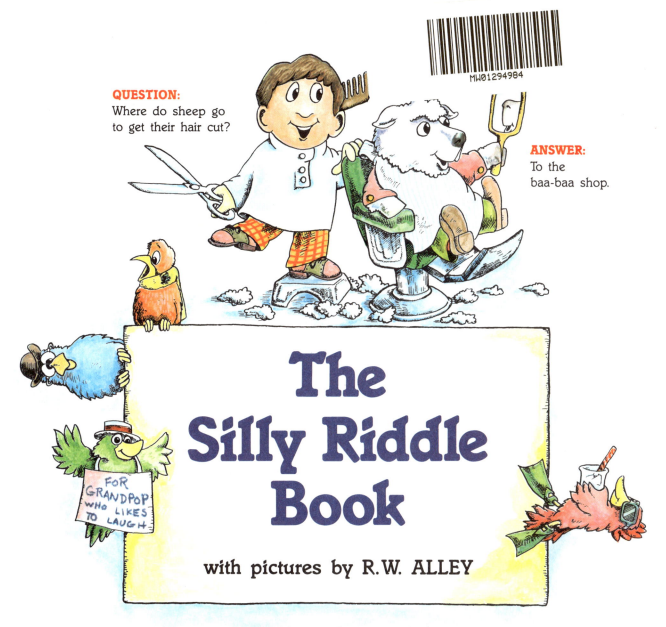

QUESTION: Where do sheep go to get their hair cut?

ANSWER: To the baa-baa shop.

The Silly Riddle Book

with pictures by R.W. ALLEY

FOR GRANDPOP WHO LIKES TO LAUGH

A Golden Book • New York
Western Publishing Company, Inc., Racine, Wisconsin 53404

Text copyright © 1981 by Western Publishing Company, Inc. Illustrations copyright © 1981 by Robert Alley. All rights reserved. Printed in the U.S.A. No part of this book may be reproduced or copied in any form without written permission from the publisher. GOLDEN®, GOLDEN & DESIGN, A GOLDEN LOOK-LOOK® BOOK, and A GOLDEN BOOK® are trademarks of Western Publishing Company, Inc. Library of Congress Catalog Card Number: 80-84788 ISBN 0-307-11860-6/ISBN 0-307-61860-9 (lib. bdg.)

QUESTION:
What's gray and has a tail and a trunk?

ANSWER:
A mouse going on vacation.

QUESTION:
Why did the girl tiptoe past the medicine cabinet?

ANSWER:
She didn't want to wake up the sleeping pills.

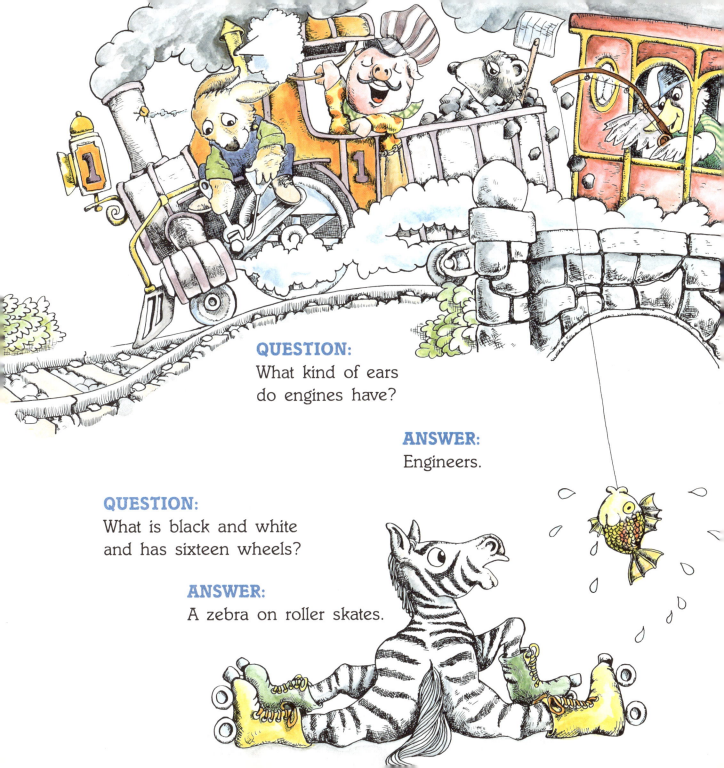

QUESTION:
What kind of ears do engines have?

ANSWER:
Engineers.

QUESTION:
What is black and white and has sixteen wheels?

ANSWER:
A zebra on roller skates.

QUESTION:
How do you keep a skunk from smelling?

ANSWER:
Hold its nose.

QUESTION:
What looks like one half of a pizza?

ANSWER:
The other half.

QUESTION:
What do you call a cat that eats lemons?

ANSWER:
A sour puss.

QUESTION:
What do you call a witch in the desert?

ANSWER:
A sand-witch.

QUESTION:
What did the elephant do when he hurt his toe and couldn't walk?

ANSWER:
He called a toe truck.

QUESTION:
How do you stop a mouse from squeaking?

ANSWER:
Oil it.

QUESTION:
What stays hot in the refrigerator?

ANSWER:
Mustard.

QUESTION:
What kind of dog has no tail and doesn't bark?

ANSWER:
A hot dog.

QUESTION:
What's the best kind of fish to have with peanut butter?

ANSWER:
Jelly fish!

QUESTION:
When are cooks cruel?

ANSWER:
When they beat the eggs and whip the cream.

QUESTION:
What would you have if you put six ducks in a box?

ANSWER:
A box of quackers.

QUESTION:
What's green with red spots?

ANSWER:
A pickle with measles.

QUESTION:
What two things can you never have for breakfast?

ANSWER:
Lunch and dinner.

QUESTION:
What's orange and falls off walls?

ANSWER:
Humpty Pumpkin.

QUESTION:
What room has no doors, no walls, no floor, and no ceiling?

ANSWER:
A mushroom.

QUESTION:
What weighs 1,000 pounds and sings?

ANSWER:
Two 500-pound canaries.

QUESTION:
What has teeth but never eats?

ANSWER:
A comb.

QUESTION:
What has arms and legs but no head?

ANSWER:
A chair.

QUESTION:
What kind of suit does a duck wear?

ANSWER:
A duck-sedo.

QUESTION:
Why was the belt arrested?

ANSWER:
Because it held up a pair of pants.

QUESTION:
What kind of shoes are made from banana peels?

ANSWER:
Slippers.

QUESTION:
Why did the chicken cross the road?

ANSWER:
To get to the other side.

QUESTION:
Why did the chicken cross the playground?

ANSWER:
To get to the other slide.

QUESTION:
What did the astronaut see on the stove?

ANSWER:
An unidentified frying object.

QUESTION:
What do you put on a pig when it burns itself?

ANSWER:
Oink-ment.

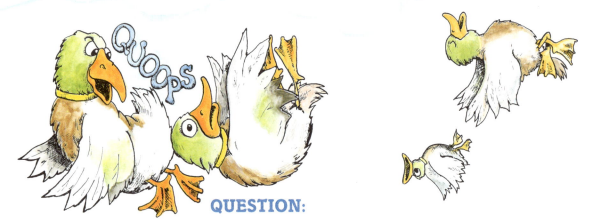

QUESTION:
What happens to ducks when they fly upside-down?

ANSWER:
They quack up.

QUESTION:
What do hippopotamuses have that no other animals have?

ANSWER:
Baby hippopotamuses.

QUESTION:
What's white on the outside, green on the inside, and hops?

ANSWER:
A frog sandwich.

QUESTION:
What ride do ghosts like best at the amusement park?

ANSWER:
The roller ghoster.